FLOORED MASTERPIECES
with Worse Verse

Spike Milligan and Tracey Boyd

Contents

To Dan from Tracey

Acknowledgments

Tracey Boyd would like to thank the following for kindly lending paintings for reproduction in this book, and for their extraordinary patience: Simon Langton for *The Duke of Urbino* and *The Duchess of Urbino*; Napier Marten for *Portrait of the Artist's Mother, Gilles* and *Bathers, Asnières*; Viviana for *The Toilet of Venus*; Andrew Kimpton for *La Goulue at the Moulin Rouge*.

Text copyright © Spike Milligan Productions Limited 1985
Illustrations copyright © Tracey Boyd 1985

First published 1985 by
MACMILLAN LONDON LIMITED
4 Little Essex Street London WC2R 3LF
and Basingstoke

Associated companies in Auckland, Delhi, Dublin, Gaborone, Hamburg, Harare, Hong Kong, Johannesburg, Kuala Lumpur, Lagos, Manzini, Melbourne, Mexico City, Nairobi, New York, Singapore and Tokyo

British Library Cataloguing in Publication Data
Milligan, Spike
    Floored masterpieces with worse verse
    I. Title   II. Boyd, Tracey
    821'.914   PR6063.13777
    ISBN 0–333–39314–7

Typeset by Bookworm Typesetting Ltd., Manchester
Printed in Hong Kong

after Caravaggio; original in the Uffizi, Florence

Bacchus

It's known the family of the apes
Do anything for pears and grapes,
So while this chimp's
Disguised as Bacchus
There's little chance
He will attack us.

after Jean-François Millet; original in the Louvre, Paris

The Gleaners

Three little cow girls
Working on a farm,
This outdoor work
Wouldn't do you any harm,
Except perhaps
A sudden attack,
A crippling pain
In the small of your back,
And of course
In this damp area
A sudden bout
Of cerebral malaria,
Then a touch
Of bovine TB,
A mild attack
Of dysentry.
Another thing
Gives one the shudders
Is getting splinters
In the udders,
And climbing over
Rural styles
Can put more splinters
In your piles,
And working on
The land, you see,
You must beware
Of leprosy.
Apart from that
There is no harm
Gleaning barley
On the farm.

Portrait of the Artist's Mother

What hi! What ho!
What a carry on crow.
(She is Whistler's mother you know)
So he has really done his best
For somebody born up in a nest.
Until now I thought that she
Was *homo sap*: like you and me.
The size of her bill, dare I say it?
I'm glad that *I* don't have to pay it.
She looks so placid on this page
But she can fly into a rage,
She can fly into a tree
Or over Leeds and Coventry.
From her history we now know
She is an American crow.
Unlike her cousin the Limey
She never says 'Caw Blimey'.
Thus ends the poem on Whistler's mother
— I never want to write another.

after James Abbot McNeill Whistler; original in the Louvre, Paris

Bathers, Asnières

There's pisches in the water,
More pisches on the grass,
Then pisches in a rowing boat!
A very pisch en pass.

Pisches out of water
'Don't live very long',
Words from the Icthyologist —
Wrong! Wrong! Wrong!!!

But! while these little pisches
Take their evening dips,
Let them make the best of
Here comes a man with the chips.

after Georges-Pierre Seurat; original in the National Gallery, London

Sacred and Profane Love

Oh what a terrible strain
To the body and brain
Is love sacred and profane.
The one from sex will abstain,
The other will do it again and again,
Even in the pouring rain.

after Titian; original in the Borghese Gallery, Rome

Observe the skunk on the right.
Well, she's been doing it all night,
Unlike the other one in white —
Unless some skunk his troth will plight
And only then she might, she might,
Say once a week, on Friday night.

Finally I now disclose
To you what may seem otiose —
Skunks make love without clothes!
But, owing to the pong that flows,
With a clothes peg on their nose
To stop them going comatose.

The Toilet of Venus
('The Rokeby Venus')

'What are you trying to do to us?'
Should be the cry of this walrus.
Let us hope that no one's seen us
Posing as the Rokeby Venus.
But let's admit it's very nice
Escaping from Antarctic ice,
Not slithering across the floes
From harpoon-wielding Eskimos.
This is the perfect hideaway,
Posing for Señor Velazquez.

The Rokeby Walrus

after Diego Velazquez; original in the National Gallery, London

Portrait of King Henry VIII

Oh what a terrible sight to see
This version of King Henry.
You will observe — he is a bull-dog,
And by his girth — a very full-dog.
I would say, this bluff King Hal
Had just had twenty tins of Pal.
Considering his gluttony and lust
I'd say this portrait's fairly just,
Considering the fact that he
Chopped ladies' heads off frequently.
A canine King made great demands,
You had to bow-wow to his commands.
Except, of course, Sir Thomas More —
Soon his head too went on the floor.
So this painting by Holbein,
I'd give it, say, a 5 point 9.

after Hans Holbein; original in the Galleria Nazionale, Rome

When Will
You Marry Me?

Seen here in Tahiti
A buffalo and his sweetie,
One of Gauguin's masterpieces,
Every day the price increases —
A million pounds at Sotheby's!
Would bring most of us to our knees.
Surely everybody knows
It's cheaper to buy two buffalos.
Gauguin — an eccentric chap
Went out there and caught the clap.
Think of the expensive fare
He paid to go and catch it there.
The fool! he could have got it free
Back at his home in Gay Paree.

NAFEA Faaipoipo

after Paul Gauguin; original in the Kunstmuseum, Basle

A Woman Bathing in a Stream

Woman bathing in a stream?
Never, never. Scream, scream, scream.
Who would want to pay to see
Such artistic traversity?
This portrait then by Rembrandt
Is very hard to understandt!
This 'woman' is a common stork,
Legs so thin she bare can walk.
But wait! Of course! I should have seen —
She's advertising margarine.
Now I can tell Stork from butter —
One can fly but not the utter.

after Rembrandt; original in the National Gallery, London

after Piero della Francesca; original in the Uffizi, Florence

The Duchess of Urbino

Oh duckie Duchess of Urbino,
Flora floriat Florentino,
Was it just a bit of luck
The Duke chose to espouse a duck?
Did you leave the local lake
To win and woo the ducal drake?
Why are you painted
Facing away?
Had you had
A row that day?
How then did you
Answer back?
Was it 'Shut up!'
Or 'Quack quack quack'?

The Duke of Urbino

Duke of Urbino,
Have you been drinking vino?
You're the most absurd duke
I ever have seeno.
Very unwise!
If you played cricket
You'd be out for a duck
On the perfect wicket.
You must have laboured
Very hard
To reach such high office
As a canard.
But steer clear of
The culinary scene,
Or you'll end up
In a
Tureen.

after Piero della Francesca; original in the Uffizi, Florence

The Three Graces

Is someone trying to get cheap laughs
With one – two – three Maasai giraffes?
In this picture – there are traces –
What used to be the Three Graces.
The only Graces known to me
Were Gracie Fields and Grace Kelly;
The only other I could trace
Was someone called Amazing Grace.
They say as 'ow I do 'ear tell
T'was copied from a Raphael.
The ones each side have just been sniffin'
What seems to be a Cox's Pippin.
Are they donkeys in pyjamas
Doing a plug for apple farmers?
Whatever it is they've gone too far –
The beasts belong in Africa.

after Raphael; original in the Musée Condé, Chantilly

The Musicians in the Orchestra

I'm telling you
That it is wrote
You'll get no music
From a goat.
You'll just get
A bleating noise
From these caprean
Hoi-polois.
It is a musical disgrace
To ask a goat
To play the bass.
Some goats can play
The pipes of Pan
Provided that
One half is man.
And that stage greenery
No doubt
They'll eat before
The night is out.
And if the audience
Shouts 'Encore',
They'll then proceed
To eat the score.

after Edgar Degas; original in the Städelsches Kunstinstitut, Frankfurt

Girl with a Pearl Earring

Oh dear, oh dear,
Someone else, I fear,
Has been messing around
With a Vermeer.
This used to be
A pretty girl
Bedecked with a lustrous creamy pearl,
But now some loony
Senza nous
Has drawn her as
A ruddy mouse,
And the pearl you see
On the opposite photo
Might even be
A Mickey Moto.

after Johannes Vermeer; original in the Koninklijk Cabinet van Schilderijen 'Mauritshuis', The Hague

Birth of Venus

Oh potty potty Botticelli,
Never ever on your Nelly,
How can you very so demean us
With this loony birth of Venus?
1 – 2 – 3 – 4 Hippopotamus,
Each one with a heavy bottomus,
Standing in that delicate shell –
Will it support her? Will it hell!
She'll never make it to the shore!
She'll plummet to the ocean floor!
She'll end up in some delta flood
Wallowing in Niger mud.
Oh no, this painting's been destroyed!
With too much Hippopotamoid.

after Sandro Botticelli; original in the Uffizi, Florence

after Sir John Everett Millais; original in the Royal Academy of Arts, London

Bubbles

You can blow up globes of hope
With a pipe and bar of soap;
Blowing transi-lucent bubbles
Can distract us from our troubles,
So landlord fill the flowing bowl
With carbolic and some hyperbole.
See above! one bubble lingers —
Will he pop it with fish fingers?
But why did they choose to employ
Some kind of fish and not a boy?
Perhaps the whole thing is a wheeze
To save him from MacFisheries.

St George
and the Dragon

Here comes Sir K'newt to kill the Dragon
Upon a horse (tho' he's still on the wagon).
He's poked his lance in the monster's eye
And hopes to make the creature die.
The damsel stands there trembling mute
For she's been missed-missed as a newt.
Sir K'newt has galloped from afar
To stop her being steak tartare
And after such a daring save
The least she can give is a micro-wave.

after Paolo Uccello; original in the National Gallery, London

La Goulue
at the Moulin Rouge

Hooray, hooray
For la Goulue,
Shaking her legs in scarlet display.
Every colour, shade and fleck
Was done by Henri Toulouse-Lautrec.
At the Moulin Rouge,
Where the place is huge,
They call him 'le petit short-arse stooge';
Even at the Concert Ball
He still looks very, very small.
He sees la Goulue
As a rose among thistles
Who's been driven mad
By French wolf-whistles

after Henri de Toulouse-Lautrec; original (poster) in the Cabinet des Estampes, Paris

Doge
Leonardo
Loredan

This Doge by Bellini
Is a foxy-faced meany.
I wonder, I wonder
Just where has he beeny?
Was he being hunted,
Fleeing in fear?
Being helped to escape
By a gondolier?
Those red-coat huntsmen
From the Quorn
Must wonder where
The hell he's gone.
Horses and hounds
All having to swim,
They'll all catch typhoid —
But not him!
They know to chickens
He is a menace,
To them the Doge means
Death in Venice.

after Giovanni Bellini; original in the National Gallery, London

after Albrecht Dürer; original in the Prado, Madrid

Self-Portrait

Why yes, of course,
But what a sauce —
This Albrecht Dürer
Is a horse!
Horses usually appear nude,
But this one obviously thinks that's rude.
Is it a gelding? Heaven knows!
How can you tell with all those clothes!
It could turn out to be a filly
(That's a horse without a willy).
Historical notes say Albrecht Dürer
Died four hundred years before the Führer.
What more can one say
Except it's time to gallop away?

Virgin and Child
with St Anne

You must believe me (if you can),
This is the Madonna and St Anne.
I used to be an aficionado
Of the late Leonardo,
But this once classical Madonna
Has a beak and feathers growing on her.
Poor Jesus Christ (whose mother this is)
Now has a mum who honks and hisses.
Perhaps he meant it as a joke
Or for the pâté-de-foie-gras folk;
If so, Pope John would not agree
With Leonardo da Vinci.

after Leonardo da Vinci; original in the Louvre, Paris

'The Ancient of Days'
(Frontispiece to Europe: A Prophecy)

If this is a painting
Signed by Blake,
Most likely then
It is a fake.
This 'God Creating the Universe'
Would make the Almighty curse and curse.
Perhaps it's the result
Of a casual meeting
'Twixt the Creator
And the late Tom Keating.
If the Bible rings true
Then God is Jewish,
But as Felix Leo
That's something newish.
The thought of God
As a Jewish lion
Could mean the end
Of the House of Zion.

after William Blake; original in the Fitzwilliam Museum, Cambridge

Le Déjeuner
sur l'Herbe

Manet is the root of all evil
Painting things like this.
It's no use — there's no excuse —
He must have been Brahms and Liszt.
He took the art world by surprise,
Exhibited in Paree:
'Naked at a picnic, Sir?'
Signed, Yours Disgustedly!
As if it wasn't bad enough,
Those naked girls are pigs!
That's not real hair
They've got up there,
They're wearing piggy-wigs!
Le Déjeuner sur l'Herbing —
I find it really most disturbing.

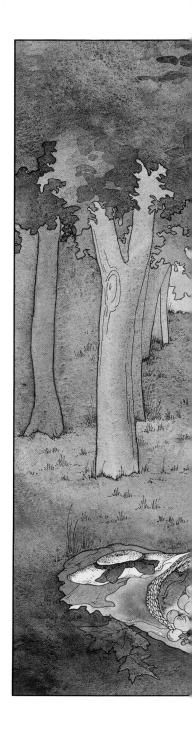

after Edouard Manet; original in the Jeu de Paume, Paris

after Thomas Gainsborough; original in the Iveagh Bequest, Kenwood, London

Mary, Countess of Howe

Amazing lady
Dressed in white,
Have you been on
The piss all night?
Your title says
'Countess of Howe',
We know that you got it
But how, girl, how?
How did the King
And courtiers cope
With a dressed up
Antelope?
To try and wed
A young gazelle
The Count he must
Have run like hell.
So, dear Mary,
Countess of Howe,
How do we
Address you now?
The safest way
It would appear
Isn't 'M'Lady'
But 'Hello, Deer'.

The Judgment of Paris

Here we see three
Very bear girls
Clad in coats of
Fleece white curls.
Being covered in
Woolly hair,
Are these bears then
Really bare?
If they're not
This could embarrass
The polar bear that's
Playing Paris.
To win that rosy
Cox's Pippin
You're only supposed
To wear your ski-in.

after Peter Paul Rubens; original in the National Gallery, London

Woman with a Fan

Hey there, Modigliani,
Are you trying to be fani?
This girl — or rather alligator —
Why in heaven did you create her?
No man in marriage
Her hand would choose,
Except to make
A pair of shoes.
Perchè — perchè
Questa pittura,
Questa donna
Senza un' futura?

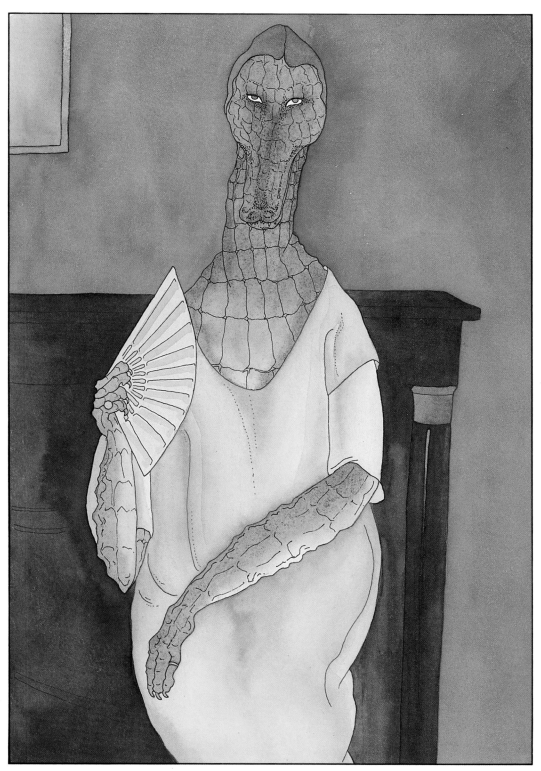

after Amedeo Modigliani; original in the Musée d'Art Moderne de la Ville de Paris

The Swing

Oh, it's very, very, very hard
To recognise this Fragonard.
It's Fragonard to try and see
What it's Fragon meant to be.
Originally 'Girl on a Swing'
And meant to be a sweet young thing,
But, Golly Gosh,
I'll eat my hat
If that is not
A pussy cat.
And down below
With eye that flickers
A Tom cat looking
Up her knickers!
That's what those froggies
Like to see
At the French
Academy.

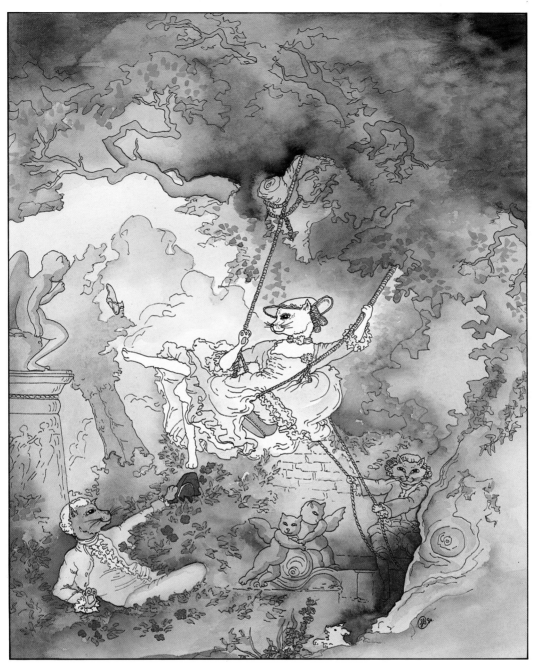

after Jean-Honoré Fragonard; original in the Wallace Collection, London

The Laughing Cavalier

Oh Laughing Cavalier, pray!
Whatever made you turn this way?
I thought that you and Frans Hals
Were pals.
When his mother saw
What you had painted
She called her advocate
Then fainted.
It's worse than any critic feared,
He omitted your moustache and beard!
How was his mind
So overtaken?
Was he fond
Of ham or bacon?
Oh dear, oh dear, oh dear, oh dear!
How sad this laughing cavalier.

Envoi

Bought by a Rajah at Sotheby's
Lac after lac he paid in rupees,
But since you've changed
Into a boar
Ten quid is all I'd pay,
No more.

after Frans Hals; original in the Wallace Collection, London

after Jan van Eyck; original in the National Gallery, London

'The Arnolfini Marriage'

Now what's this?
Ah! wedded bliss,
A local Mister and his Miss.
But underneath that big black hat
I see the features of a rat!
The lady in the light green dress
Turns out to be a coy ratess.
Oh happy, happy
Wedding morn,
Especially as she's
Three months gone.
There's a lesson to be learnt
If you don't want your fingers burnt:
Even tho' it makes her ill
Put your girlfriend on the pill,
Or else her father will be at you
You — you dirty rat you!

Les Demoiselles d'Avignon

Au grin girl-gogs goggle-goo,
Green gig gog-frogs fraggle-froo,
Six sex Saxen shuckle sheen
Sush such sex saw — bottle green.
Pic-pic-ahso — pick-pick-poo,
Ah-pic — ah-pic — ah-tish-oo.
Bare bom bosoms,
Twi tits-too,
Hip yip — apple green — nudie doo.
Naked-knickerless you see bots,
Flesh-flish flashing — lots and lots.
Les Demoiselles d'Avignon
Standing there sans nothing on.

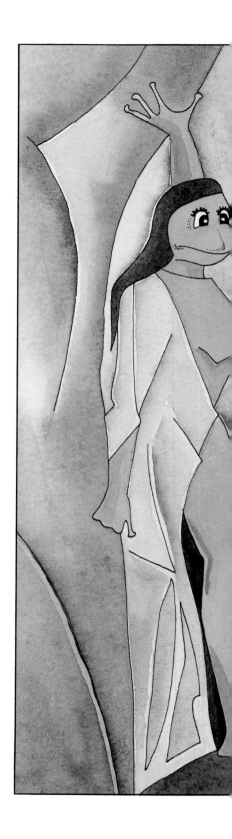

after Pablo Picasso; original in the Museum of Modern Art, New York

after Sir Anthony van Dyck; original in the Royal Collection, Windsor

The Three Heads of Charles I

Behold, behold royal canine grace —
But what a triplicated face.
One left — one right —
One in the middle —
Sing bow wow wow,
Hey-diddle-diddle.
If you look up your history books
It's not as puzzling as it looks:
When on that day he was beheaded
He had two left — so he wasn't deaded!

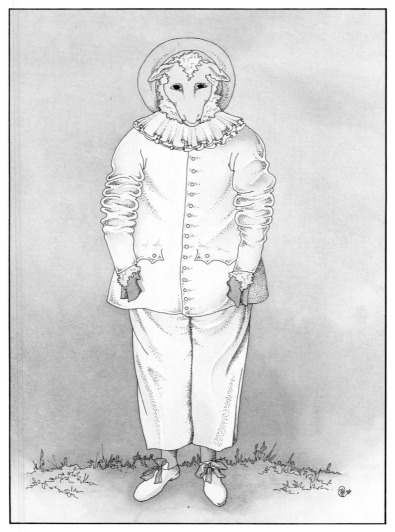

after Jean-Antoine Watteau; original in the Louvre, Paris

Gilles

This painting by Watteau!
He must have been Blotteau!
Even a glutton
Won't eat lamb dressed as mutton
This isn't Gilles,
It's just bloody silly!